Shelley Rotner &
Stephen Calcagnino

Photographs by Shelley Rotner

SCHOLASTIC INC.
New York Toronto London Auckland Sydney
Mexico City New Delhi Hong Kong Buenos Aires

THE BODY BOOK

Book design by Mina Greenstein. The text of this book is set in 29 point Futura Medium.

Printed in the U.S.A.

ISBN 0-439-40014-7

4 5 6 7 8 9 10 24 10 09 08 07 06 05 04

To everyone who shares my life

—S.R.

To Helen and Tony

—S.C.

We all have bodies with many different parts.

We have eyes to see,

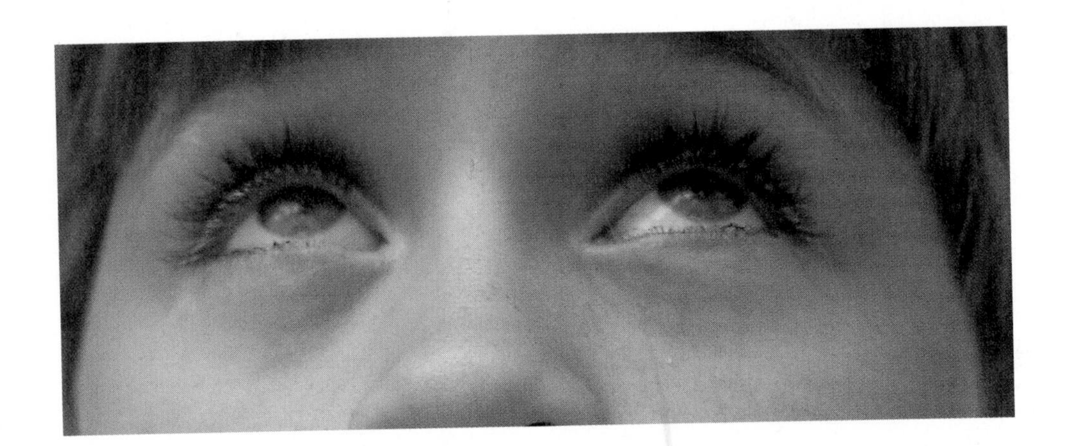

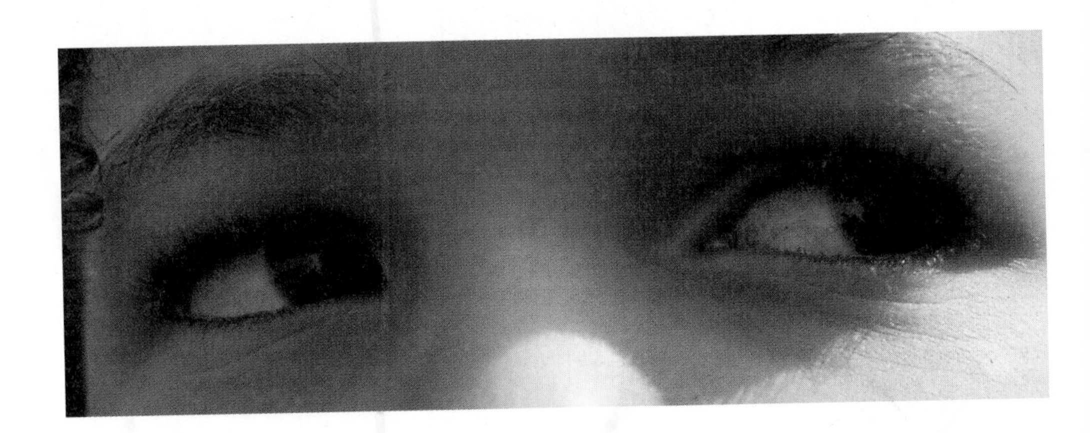

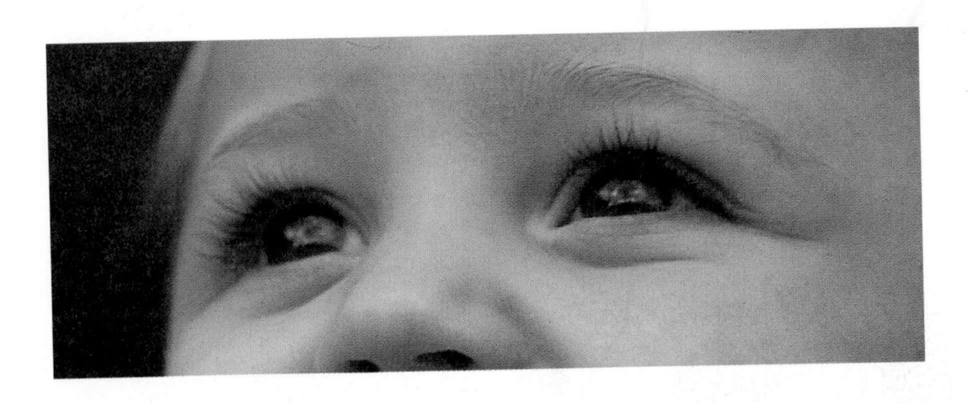

a nose to smell,

ears to hear and a mouth to talk,

tongues
to taste,

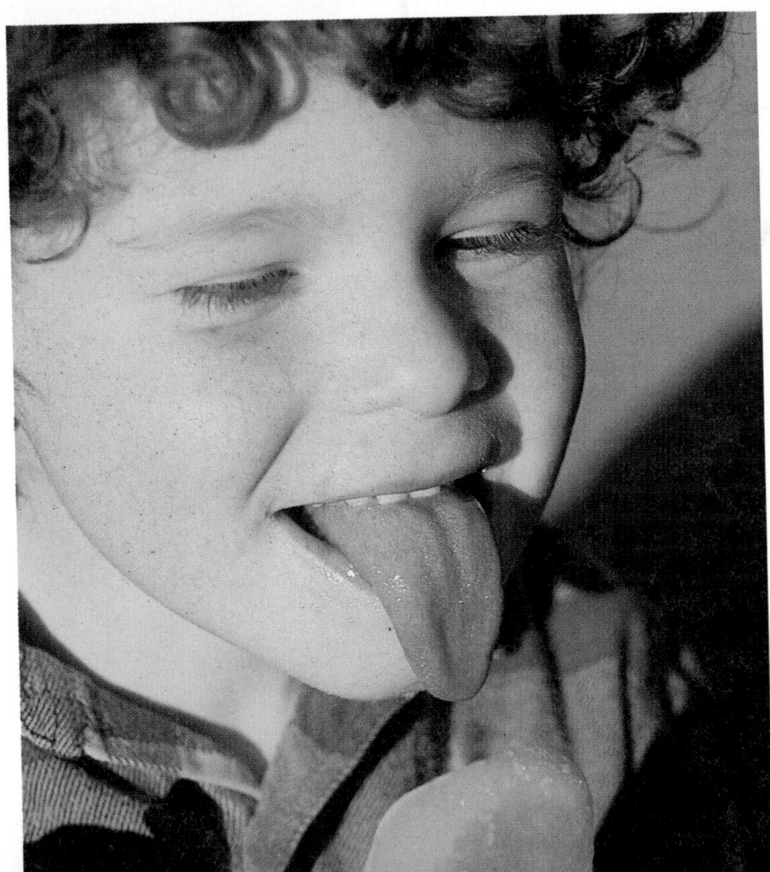

teeth to bite and chew.

Hands to touch,

arms to hug and hold,

legs and feet
to run and jump,

elbows and knees
to bend and move.

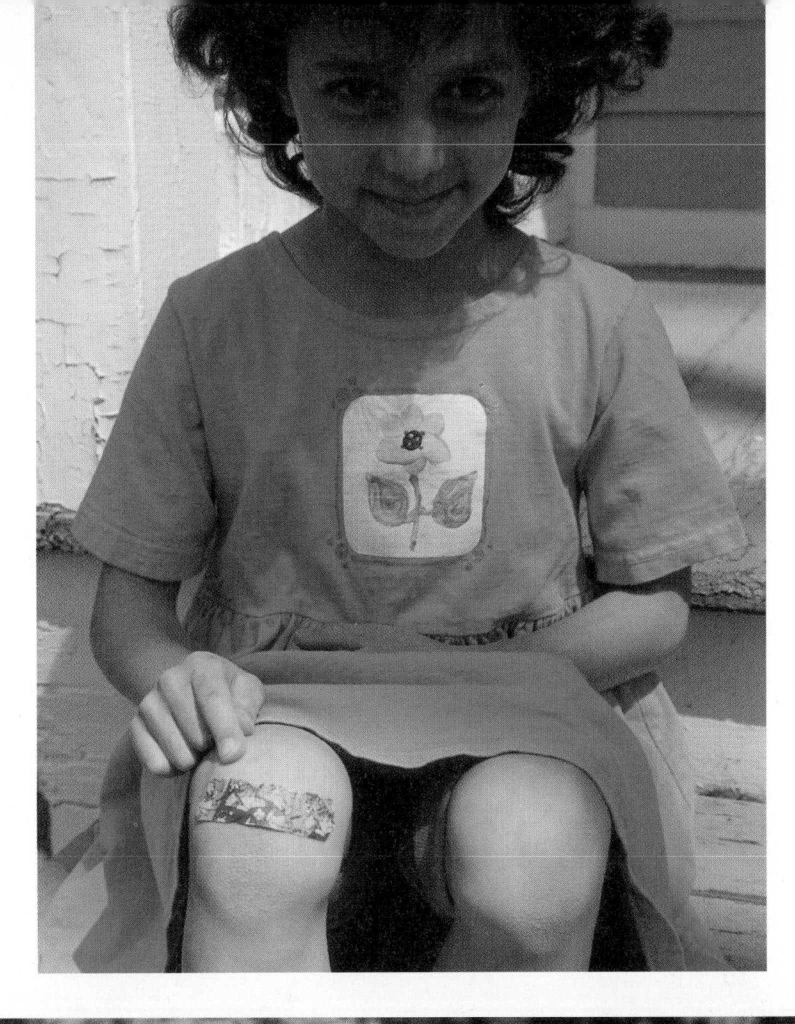

Fingers,
toes,

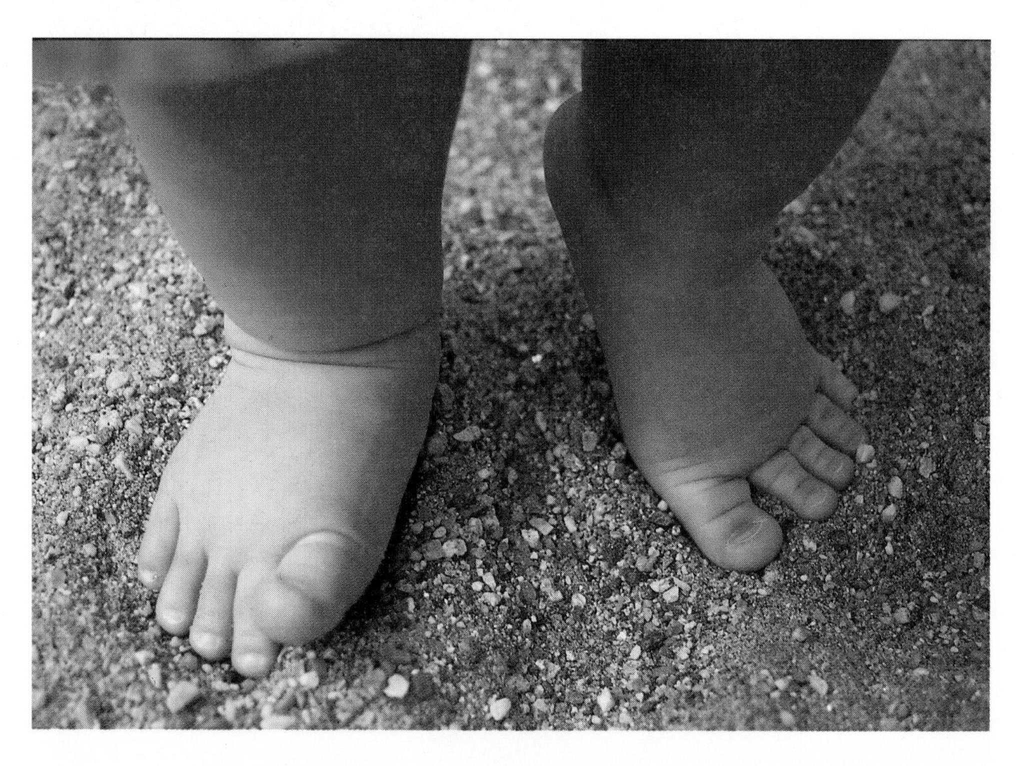

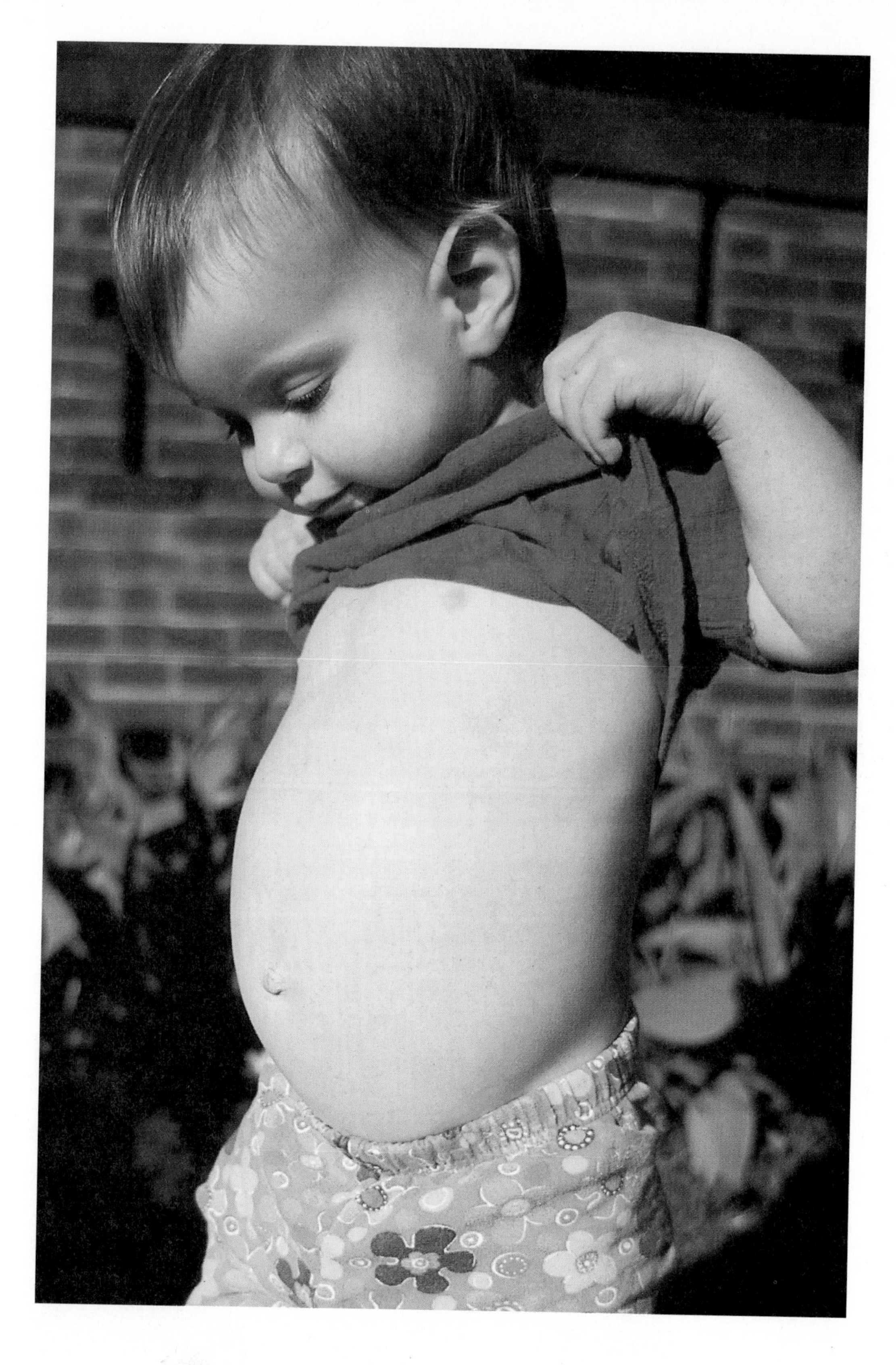

and one belly button.

SMASH
She kicks. She screams.
She wants to smash the
world to smithereens.

Our bodies can do many things.

Young, old,

big, small.

Bodies!
All shapes, colors,
and sizes.